Terms
of
Venery,
Revised

Terms of Venery, Revised

Poems

Paula J. Lambert

Sheila-Na-Gig Editions

Terms of Venery, Revised © 2025 Paula J. Lambert

Cover art: Michelle Kingdom
Exchanging Heaven for Earth, Embroidery

Cover Design: Paula J. Lambert
Cover Consultant: Ali Wade
Author photo: Paige Critcher

ISBN: 978-1-962405-44-7
Library of Congress Control Number: 2025944759

Sheila-Na-Gig Editions
Russell, KY
Hayley Mitchell Haugen, Editor
www.sheilanagigblog.com

Acknowledgments:

The following poems were previously published, some in slightly different form, by the following:

A Confluence of Poems (Poems for Tributaries Everywhere), Eighth Annual Edith Chase Poetry Anthology, 2025: "What Feeds / What Is Fed"
Autumn Sky Poetry Daily: "Ode to Understanding"
Earth: Poems of Presence and Possibility(Tiny Wren Press, 2025): "Lady Slipper"
The Guilt That Gathers (Pudding House, 2012): "The Tornado"
Gyroscope Review: "Grief As Tunnel Painted on the Side of a Mesa"
The Half Life of Echoes (Tiny Wren Press, 2024): "Snow Trillium"
Lake Effect: An International Literary Journal: "Vanitas"
The Nature of Our Times: Poems on America's Lands, Waters, Wildlife, and Other Natural Wonders: "Apologia"
Poetry Breakfast. "Bear," "Redbuds"
Quartet Journal: "Making It Easier"
Sheila-Na-Gig online: "How Many Birds," "Hydrangeas," "This Is Why the Patter of Rain"
Sinkhole (Bottlecap Press 2025): "Covenant," "Doppler Effect," "Heat," "The Next Beast," "The Only Thing Missing" "Pretending," "Sinkhole," "Sound"
Top Tweet Tuesday @Blackbaugh Poems, Twitter/X: "Terms of Venery, Revised for the Anthropocene"
Unapaulagetic. Substack: "God Considers the Next Extinction," "On All the Ways One Fractured Myth Leads Directly Into Another,""Stringfoot," "Toll Road," "On the Weight of the Soul, the Weight of a Cloud, the Weight of a Whale," "And If I Should Die by the Same Strain That Killed My Avian Brethren, Let Them Not Say"

The author would like to thank the Ohio Arts Council, the Greater Columbus Arts Council, and the Virginia Center for the Creative Arts for their support of her work. She would also like to express her gratitude for the ongoing, loving support of her husband, Michael Perkins.

for the ancestors

who suffered,
and craved,
and grieved,
and knew joy

Contents

I. The Tornado

II. Vanitas

III. Terms of Venery Revised

IV. Making It Easier

I.

The Tornado

Baby, I've been here before...

—Leonard Cohen

The Tornado

I.

When he woke, he told you, he'd heard someone asking,
Do you think anyone could have survived this?
He cried out for help. That's when he knew he was alive,
when he heard his own voice: *Help*. The people asked,
Where are you? He called back, *I don't know*.
They hollered back and forth, like children
playing Marco Polo, the only water around him
the rain still falling, the thick wet mud he was lying in.

II.

Broken in so many places, he wanted, of all things,
his back scratched. He pushed the blankets off,
lifted his gown up, and you saw the compression bandage
across his belly, penis below it, catheter attached,
his scrotum the size and color of an eggplant.
Rolling carefully onto one side so your hand could reach
his sweaty, itchy skin, he moaned when you scratched—
Don't stop—and you didn't, not till he was ready,
slowly rolling himself back into place,
lowering the gown back over the eggplant
and raising the blankets to his chest,
hiding it all, all over again.

III.

It didn't help, in your mind, that it happened
after you'd left, that you weren't there to protect him,
or die next to him, but you took comfort that the news on TV
and in the paper, keeping up with his progress for days,
never mentioned he even had a wife. If no one knew,
no one could ask why you weren't there.

IV.

Six months earlier you'd tried to die your own way,
tried to kill the chaos of guilt and debris twisting through
your brain, but it didn't work, and you were forced to say

out loud the words you thought would send you to hell:
I want a divorce. Turns out not saying it was the real hell.
Turns out a little R&R on the psych ward
wound up changing everything.
Everything's fine now, see?

V.
Dorothy's house blew away, but it didn't blow up.
Her house killed a wicked witch, but yours scarred a good man.
She found color and gold bricks and wisdom.
You found surgeons and insurance men, a wheelchair
and a way to go through with the divorce.
Dorothy got to go home again.

VI.
With nothing left, there was nothing to squabble over.
No house, no kids, no need for the lawyers. Think of it:
the hand of God made the divorce easy and cheap.
Turns out, there never was a need for forgiveness.

Hangdog

The last time I talked to my ex,
I asked him about the dog, and he said,
Didn't I tell you? The dog, it turned out,
who'd run beside the tractor a thousand times before,
one day ran in front of it. *I killed her*, he said,
and the tone of his voice told me he'd never told anyone
and knew it goddamned well, that he'd buried the dog
and tried to forget what happened.

I hated he'd used me as a way to finally confess:
Bless me, please, for I have sinned, and I'd be damned
if forgiveness was going to come from me—
I was too much like the dog.
                                    She'd come to us
a stray: skinny, groveling, a beagle/blue heeler mix
bearing the marks of training by a too-heavy hand.
We coaxed her and coaxed her and fed her till she finally gave in
and loved us, a healthy, beautiful, happy dog, we thought.
She ran away, and we found her months later
living with somebody else, living with a different name.
She came back to us but was never quite the same:
a hangdog kind of dog who knew she ought to be happy
but wasn't.
                    By then I was planning my own escape,
eyeing the tractor, too, and sure that sounds worse than it was
but I mean I wanted to die
because something was in me that wanted to live
a different life. I suffered my own sins for years
till I realized I'd done nothing wrong, leaving him,
till I realized I, too, could run free, run wild, could even make love
like a man, unburdened, unbridled, on top
of the goddamned world, and I enjoyed myself
for a while before settling down again, happy finally. Free.

I mean, what's loyalty, really—to a woman or a dog,
carefully trained or even carefully loved—

but an accident waiting to happen? I learned
I had something more sacred to offer a man than my body.
I understood, *hallelujah*, the divine nature
of what I'd once believed profane.

The Church teaches you love is something you save
for just one person. The Church, it seems, forgets how to love
the world. And I don't know what that dog believed—
I don't know, even, if she wanted to die, but I do know
sometimes you have to die to one world to learn how to live
in the next. And damn if that dog isn't the only thing
I'm sorry to have left behind. Damn if that dog didn't teach me
what it might look like to move on.

II.

Vanitas

*I moved my arms
And coughed, and in the end saw land.*

—Mary Oliver

Vanitas

I sit by the open window listening
to frogs and crickets, rotting pears

plummeting through branches and
thudding the ground. Yesterday,

the body of a starling on the back step.
The dark world offers itself. Cries out.

Come daylight, we mow the pears.
We pretend not to see, not to hear.

Doppler Effect

The echoing pulse
of what we don't want
to remember. Or face.

The Next Beast

All eyes here on the new hurricane.
Across the globe, earthquake. Yes,
it's Whack-a-Mole, we the moles,
hiding in a box of whirring gears
and thumping levers, catastrophe
the man above us, drunk and swinging
a club: WHOMP! Fire. WHOMP! Flood.
WHOMP! A new strain of disease.
Still…this: my granddaughter's first day
of school. Arms wide, smiling,
she welcomes all the new day will
bring, wearing light-up sneakers
and a brand-new unicorn backpack.
She sticks out her tongue, playfully,
for the pictures, and later, we play
puppet show. Every beast she brings
to the stage says, *Hello! I love you!*
Until she stops, leans in, whispers,
Grandma! You're my best friend! Then
the next beast growls: *I'm gonna poop
on your head!* And we laugh and laugh.

Lady Slipper

Strange, small anatomical heart
risen, on its own, from the soil.

Bear

Just past midnight, a bear
and a wolverine thrashed

through the bushes outside
our living room window.

Or maybe that god-awful
sound was just a raccoon

falling off the roof. No bears
in this part of Ohio. No

wolverines. But in the news
this morning, flamingoes

blown in from Hurricane
Idalia. I go outside, look for

fur, blood, evidence of a fight.
I was so sure something died

last night. I wondered what
flamingos might sound like,

riding a storm, landing in
a place they don't recognize

or want any part of. Might it be
anything like a bear fight, or

a raccoon tumbling through
gravity, pissed? I wonder

if the birds thrashed like that,
scream-hissing so horrifically

at what brought them here,
at how they'd landed, how

they'd get back to where they
were, to what it was like, before.

Snow Trillium

She leans in close and squints. *Do I know you?*
My heart begins to break, but she smiles, impishly.

I take her hands in mine, and we laugh. One day,
we both know, I'll have to tell her my name.

Covenant

Cracked clay soil—soon,
deluge.

The road, the empty bowl:
sinkhole.

Sinkhole

And the earth washed away beneath the road,
beneath the railroad tracks. The asphalt then

collapsed into the hole, and the iron rails, spikes.
And cars fell into the hole, and houses sometimes,

and people and people's dreams, and people's
refusal to acknowledge that what they thought

wouldn't be—couldn't be—so, was. Is. And will
be worse and worse and worse, sky so far from

the bottom of a hole, and suddenly so close,
there being no further, no deeper for us to fall.

Sound

From the open window, I can hear tires screeching—
the kind where a car is turning too sharply too fast.

Like in the movies. Where, I wonder, is there a road
close enough for that to be happening? Other nights,

I hear the train two miles away. Or cattle mooing,
or the same cattle slaughtered. Our daughter tells me

the new meds are making her hear soft rustling
sometimes, doors slamming. Babies crying. No voices,

just vague auditory hallucinations. And a friend
tells me about a terrible case of tinnitus, a long, slow

bell ringing since contracting Covid. We compare notes.
For me, it's nightmares. Something evil trying to break

through the door: I heave my weight against it, slam it
closed, wake covered in sweat, listening carefully

for what's real. I wonder if all sound might be echoes
of want, of fear, of need. If sound itself might be energy:

spirit, ghost, memory. If all soft rustling, every bell,
every beast lowing might only be asking us to concede

our collective terrible suffering: to hear, to see, to touch,
to feel. Oh, is it too much, too much, to say…to love?

Pretending

In the dry cocoon bathtub,
granddaughter in my lap,

we crack an invisible whip,
cry out: *On Dasher! On*

Dancer! We are in control
of Santa's sleigh, soaring

the evening sky, nothing
but stockings and cookies

ahead. I'm ignoring the drone
footage I saw earlier: flood

damage, the goddamned
sink holes. When she tires

of the sleigh, we move
to the glass-walled shower,

splash our hands on the still-
wet floor, pat the soap,

press our palms to the glass.
No cries here—only giggles,

her tiny handprints next to mine.
We are Paleolithic cave dwellers

leaving our mark, pretending
some part of this will last.

Balance

Columbus, OH / Leominster, MA

No water at the waterfall today.
Stagnant pools in the river it feeds.

Back home, floods. The sinkholes.
Dams and bridges collapsing. I look

for balance between the extremes,
find it in the dark, writing.

The Liminal Space
Between Home and Home

Rochester, again. Exactly halfway:
untethered from home and home,

the man who delights in every detail
of me, the mother who recalls less

and less of my life—or my siblings'
lives or hers—whose answer to nearly

every question these days is I don't
know...I don't remember...a shrug.

I'm never sure if she can't remember
or no longer cares about providing

the answers: that part of her work
is done. Mom might just be out of

fucks to give, not that she had many
to start with: lock your doors,

save your money, who are you trying
to impress? I scribble my thanks

on a pad I find in the desk, leave
five dollars for the maid, (for what?

I hear in my head), check out
of a place few will ever know I was.

For the first time in how many years,
I miss my turn back onto the thruway,

headed neither east nor west, and for
a while, I just keep going, unburdened,

unbeholden, following signs I don't
recognize to places I've never been,

wondering what my answer might be
should somebody ask me later where

I've been, what I've done, what on earth
I could possibly have been thinking.

Toll Road

On the side of the highway, a deer
shorn of its legs.

A flock of birds rising through rain
in perfect unison.

We just drive, indifferent to horror
and the blur of miracles.

Guano

When I read the news that four previously unknown colonies of Emperor Penguins were discovered through satellite images of their poop, enormous brown stains on the Antarctic ice, all I could think was this: It's official. There's no place left on earth to hide.

The Only Thing Missing

All is loss, my children. All is love.
The only thing missing is peace in our hearts.

Let go of what you thought the world was.
Reach out to what the world is.

III.

Terms of Venery, Revised

say to them:
"I am not ashamed..."

—Wendell Berry

God Considers the Next Extinction

Sifting through the world's detritus—
fallen trees, broken people, so many birds—
I think what a fine experiment this was,
busy beavers gnawing endlessly, creating dams and lodges,
eco systems unto themselves till it was all too much,
a nuisance for all involved, and they died
by their own successful hand.

(You were the beavers, dear ones,
naughty ones. See all the destruction you caused?)

I run my fingers through tepid ocean waters,
feel how much has accumulated on the cluttered ocean floor:
fish bones, bleached coral—I run my thumb
down the length of an anxious blue whale's back, still heaving.
The final gasps of so many creatures echo
under water, on land. They've collapsed
onto each other's backs, into each other's arms,
so many last words layered into the debris.

I hold the Earth in my palm, heart barely beating,
and wonder what the next extinction might be,
once she recovers, once she catches her breath
and feels herself ready to start again.

Terms of Venery
Revised for the Anthropocene

An extinction of birds,
a ghosting of whales,
a haunting of humans.

A memory of trees.
An echo of Monarchs.
A sobbing of stars.

How Many Birds

On Riverside Drive, a red-winged blackbird
    flies in front of my car. *Hello*, he says. *See me?*

In the Aldi parking lot a few days later,
    picking up groceries I didn't have time

to shop for, the young man loading my car
    says, "Wow—that's a huge crow." There it is,

on top of a tree just a few yards away.
    Once I see, it flies off in a clatter of wings

and a barking huff: *Pay attention!*
    A few days after that, I see a brown blur

over the hood of my car—cowbird, maybe,
    or sparrow, or an awkward juvenile robin.

I smash my brakes. The world tells us
    when to stay alert. How to. It tells us again

when we refuse. How kind the world
    in its infinite wisdom. How willing to sacrifice

itself. How many birds haven't I seen?
    How many more have I hit? A cardinal once:

the loud thump, the horror of her body
    wedged in the grill when I finally stopped.

Stringfoot

I.
It's the reason for so many pigeons
with missing toes: stringfoot. Human hair,
tangles of thread and yarn, dental floss.
The detritus of humans
strangling the toe, the foot, the limb
until it necrotizes and falls off.

II.
Once, I loved someone who lived on an idyllic Indiana farm.
And I loved sitting on the small back porch at sunset,
freshly bathed, drawing a paddle brush through
my wet, waist-length hair.
I loved the texture of dusk there,
the purple martins' dive and dance
through the evening's dying light. I believed
the loose strands I pulled from the hairbrush
and offered to the air were a gift. *For the nests*,
I figured, inside the huge house on its towering pole,
and I tell you now I felt so glad to be of help,
to be part of a world where, every night,
darkness fell just like this, like a billowing line-dried sheet
still scented with the breeze so even in our dreams
the birds continued to sweep those perfect, gloaming skies.

III.
The highest concentration of one-legged pigeons
in urban city centers is always near the salons.
And in that viral video of a dancing bird
bouncing to the beat of a sidewalk busker—
hashtag *happiness*
hashtag *inspiration*
hashtag *this bird is my everything*
hashtag *blurred lines*
there must have been a salon nearby:
that was a stringfoot bird.

IV.
The only pigeons where I live are mourning doves.
I know every sound they make: the mating calls,
the wing-whistle warnings. Once, suddenly,
a perfect, snow-white dove appeared in the yard
as if, somewhere, a magician had released him to my care.
And once, a friend told me about a dove in his yard—
a story, he said, only I would understand.
Crossing the yard at twilight,
carrying scraps to the can at the curb,
he saw dun-colored feathers in the grass.
On his way back, he saw more feathers,
one spotted with blood, and looked up to see a single tuft
of something *like the first flake of snow in winter*
floating down. Mesmerized, he watched
as a steady stream of feathers cascaded down all around him.
A hawk, he realized, in the branches above,
was eating its prey.

V.
My friend and I both are waiting for our mothers
to die. I know how that sounds.
It's nonetheless true. *How's your mom?*
we ask when we get together for lunch, for tea, for walks
in our back-yard gardens. *Hanging in there. How's yours?*
Those garden get-togethers started with COVID,
and we learned to ask about the cone flowers, too,
the sunflowers starting to rise, the hydrangeas
sprawling in the sun. Those first four years
had taught us a new tenderness. And another Mother,
we knew, was dying, too. We rallied, though,
when the vaccines came, and believed, for a while,
we could overcome anything. But the mourning doves,
wings whirring like drones, told us to think again.
This year, under the weight of a new torrent of terror,
spring hardly happened at all. The brown grass
gasped into green, but everything else struggling
to blossom just froze in place: yellow daffodils,

the pink blooms of the tulip magnolia, purple phlox
just starting to blush. Everything froze,
shriveling back to brown. A new spring will come,
we know, and the peonies, the bergamot,
those heavy hydrangeas. And so will the searing heat,
the wildfires, an ever-widening drought.
How's your Mother, we'll continue to ask.
Hanging in there, we'll keep saying,
for a little while longer.

VI.
The difference between pigeons and doves
is negligible. Mostly, the doves are smaller.
Pigeons, people think, are disease-ridden birds,
rats with wings, while doves are somehow symbols
of hope. A few years back, in New York City,
walking through Washington Square Park,
our son showed us where he sometimes plays chess,
we listened to jazz, saw so many artists
selling prints of their work and plein air painters
working in real time. When I sat on a bench
to watch the pigeons for a while, I tried to see them
as anything but ordinary birds, oil-slick gray,
necks bobbing like chickens, weirdly wide-open eyes
holding only the blankest of stares.
I wondered how Tesla could have fallen in love
except that, by then, Nikola Tesla was crazy.
When I rejoined the family, we wandered
to the dog park, saw so many expensive breeds,
and I marveled at the sculpted gardens close by,
flowers brilliantly in bloom and, it turned out,
forming an elegant entryway for the public rest rooms.
You don't want to go in there, our son said,
turning away, and when I asked him why,
he laughed. *You just don't.* He'd used the men's room
just once, he said, and *you can't believe
how backed up it was. Shit everywhere. The smell.*
Here's the thing, though—and not just about the bathrooms

in Washington Square Park.
People need to drop their shit somewhere,
physically, metaphorically, or more than toilets
back up. More than the not-enough mental health facilities,
more than the too-many gun shops and shooting galleries.
Public parks and public schools, shopping malls
and movie theaters are filled with people
carrying their shit like so many stringfoot birds,
bearing the burden of what nobody wanted
to deal with. Losing parts of themselves
because nobody—even people like me
with the best of intentions—had any idea what to do.

VII.
My favorite park here is at Antrim Lake.
My friend and I go off the main trail
by parting the branches of invasive honeysuckle
and walking instead on the wooded path that follows the river
and opens to a beautiful, barren flood plain.
The trees there, some of them, are covered in poison ivy,
but the ivy only grows as far as people are tall,
as high as people can reach. So we keep our distance
and study the trees by looking up:
the bark helps us parse the various oaks and maples,
cottonwoods, hackberry, slippery elm,
and when we're not sure, we look higher
studying the crowns where green leaves shimmer
and wave against the light of brilliant blue skies.
Our favorite trees by far are the sycamores,
silver-white, holy Mothers indeed,
guarding the banks like queens. My favorite birds
at Antrim Park are the Great Blue Herons,
less plentiful than the geese and mallards,
harder to find, but there, with the robins and cardinals,
sparrows and finches, flickers sometimes,
and migrating warblers, red-winged blackbirds
and, always, always, the delicate doves
named for the sound that resembles our sorrow,

loved for signifying that which we hold most sacred.
And separate, somehow,
from what we consider diseased.

VIII.
No one wants to see a dove die.
But no one, really, wants to fault the hawk its meal.
That's nature, we say. The way the world works.
It happens every day. No one wants to see
a stringfoot pigeon lose a toe, a foot, a leg.
It's not the same as the hawk, but still, no one believes
anything they've done could possibly be to blame.
But the suffering of stringfoot birds
is wholly preventable. There's no one to blame but us.
Our hair, our wigs, our weaves,
our ribbons and thread and yarn,
that floss we use to clean our teeth every day.
Our trash, blowing about the streets and sidewalks
and killing more than the birds. No one wants to watch
their Mother die. We're doing it just the same.
We see the bloody tell-tale signs,
we turn our heads away. We know the dove is dying,
but hashtag *love* to tell ourselves the bird is hashtag *dancing.*
Hashtag *I'm fine. It's fine. Everything's fine.*
I'm not sure why we're so afraid
to drop our shit and say it's not.
To say *I see it now. I'm sorry.*
We carry our pain like threads of hair
tangled around our hearts, anger like floss knotting our nerves.
Grief and sadness, the loss of hope?
That's just one bird eating another.
We're the walking wounded—
we're the birds in mourning.

IX.
Nikola Tesla wasn't crazy
when he fell in love with a bird.
He said, *I understood her, and she understood me.*

If we all understood what the birds are telling us,
what the birds are showing us,
we all might come to understand love at its finest.
We all might come to understand death,
in its natural course, as a blessing.
We might come to understand
the suffering we inflict on each other
is something that binds us all.
That the bounty of birds winging their way across the planet
are migrating versions of you and of me.
That when one bird's in trouble, we all are.
When one bird takes flight, we all do.
When one bird calls, we all can answer.
When one bird sings, our throats, together,
can open to complete the chorus
that greets the dawn of a brand-new day,
and together, at dusk, as the day is closing,
we can dive and dance through the gloaming.

What Anglers Are Calling the Spins

In the news today: fish spiraling
in the Florida keys, a frightening phenomenon
found in dozens of species, cause unknown,
likely neurotoxins from a single-cell algae
living on seaweed. Multiply that
by generalized pollution, super-heated
waters…I know this dance, the weight
of these dark waters.
                        A childhood friend,
I just learned, died alone in his garage after drinking
his way through an unchecked, manic year—
really, let's face it—an unchecked manic life.
I loved him. His laugh. His stories. Hey
remember when? Story after story I don't remember
from our childhood. The lake! You don't remember
the lake? The only lake I remember, I tell him,
is the one where I almost drowned,
where my father ran into the water
to save me.
                And my sister tells me
the priest from our parish, who died of cancer in 1979—
too young! we all wept, and built a cemetery shrine—
has been posthumously convicted of molesting a child.
It might have been me. It might have been
pretty much anyone I knew, growing up. How many
of us have spun our way through these depths,
through how many toxins, seeking redemption,
pleading forgiveness, coming to rest at last—
peace at last—in how many empty,
lonely garages?
                        Bile in my belly for days now,
processing daily updates, all this news
of poison fish, holy fish, I wake with a migraine.
Excruciating, exquisite pain, the world itself
in a manic cycle: rain, hail, sunlight, snow:
April in Ohio. Back home, the earth quakes

beneath its own new blanket of blizzard white.
My sister sends me a photo: snow-capped crocus.
Purple vestments peaking through.
I don't tell her what I dreamt last night.
The weight on top of me.
How I gasped for air.
                                  Listen: about those fish?
That single-cell algae? Everything vile fights for its life.
Innocence writhes an unholy dervish, startlingly aware
that death is an awful birth to the exact same world
made suddenly clear and blindingly beautiful:
a crystal spike through the brain's third eye. I know
by now how migraines work, melting back into bile
churning its way through my colon. Eventually, I flush it away.
Clarity comes, and the world made new clambers
for words floating in like a new infection.
I think of the sawfish I saw on the news,
critically endangered, floundering
on a Florida ocean flash—
what anglers are calling the spins.
                                  Listen.
All these words, clambering now? All this
new news, old news? I know the importance of writing it down.
I know the danger of spin.

Terms of Venery
Revised for the Church

A perdition of priests,
an agony of acolytes,
a prozac of progeny.

Powder Down

Call it an imprint, what remains
of the dove when it hits the glass.
A reverse negative. It's something you don't forget
when you see it. The first time, I was sure
it was proof of God—proof, at least, of the holy.
Maybe you thought that, too.

Hidden below some birds' breast feathers
are patches of down that never molt: they grow
and grow until the tips break down
into dust. (Remember that you are dust,
and to dust you shall return…)
Some birds claw that talc back into their feathers
as they preen.

When a dove careens into what they never saw
coming, what they didn't know
was a reflection of sky solid as stone,
they leave that residue behind.
Some birds recover.
Some birds don't.

Here are two stories. First, the snow-white dove
in my yard this summer, released
at a wedding, maybe, or from a magician's hat,
or escaped from a cage in somebody's suburban home.
He leapt from the weedy brush I walked through,
landed on my neighbor's roof,
let me watch him from there. I took his picture.
I still might have thought it a dream
had my husband not told me later
he'd seen the bird from the window.
We never saw him again. I looked. Years ago,
there was a bird I never saw,
who left his imprint on the glass.

It's something you don't forget.
I was sure it was proof of God—proof, at least, of the holy.
Maybe you thought that, too.

Maybe I was the bird. Maybe you were.
Maybe He was.
Maybe I was what was left behind. Or you were.
Or He was.

Maybe the dove who came to my yard escaped.
Maybe he was asking for forgiveness.
Maybe the bird had a genetic mutation
and was snatched by the hawk I've seen lurking before.
So be it.

A flock of doves is sometimes called a pitying.
A flock of doves is sometimes called a flight.
What remains of the dove when it hits the glass
is no mystery. What remains of the dove
has a name.

On All the Ways One Fractured Myth
Leads Directly Into Another

I.
When a dust storm in Texas rained down as mud
here in central Ohio, it surprised pretty much everyone
waking up to filthy cars and weirdly streaked windows.
I mean, it wasn't the butterfly effect any of us ever imagined,
but was close enough to the hazy, smoke-scented skies we had
during those crazy Canadian wildfires—
that went on for weeks. And of course we worried about Canada,
but mostly we wanted not to think at all about what besides trees
had been incinerated, bird and animal particulates
floating overhead, filling our lungs and clogging the filters
of our fancy new in-home air filtration systems. Brand new.
Every disaster, you know, spawns a good old-fashioned capitalist
spending spree. It's what we're best at,
and the lines at the local car washes were long
after that goddamned *dirty rain*. What's an American to do
but hose things down, bracing for the next disaster?

II.
So it seems, historically speaking, that the sirens of old
were bird-women, not mermaids as falsely translated by men
for hundreds of years. And anyway,
the mermaids early explorers thought were real
were manatees. Pardon me for parsing the metaphor—
if one exists at all—that a Texas dust-storm mud rain
might be anything like discovering mermaids are sea cows
and sea cows once women with wings, but didn't we once believe
in the promise of pure-blue skies, that the breath of the world
carrying Monarchs to Mexico and guiding hummingbirds home
was actually something good, with the power to heal us all
if we let ourselves breathe deep and slow? And sure,
we've known about acid rain for years, and sure,
the urban among us who ever lived anywhere near a steel mill
are familiar with the soot that used to collect on our windowsills.

But still we believed something pure was out there somewhere,
in what some of us used to call the wild blue yonder.

III.
Anyway, as to pure, have you seen the viral video
of that turtle born with its heart outside its shell?
A tiny, rapidly beating heart open to the world
like a throbbing clitoris, a heart that said, *This is me,*
this is what's inside the twin shields of my being,
this is what keeps me alive.
The turtle's name was Hope. Hope died last year
at the same time the lunar lander christened Athena
crashed into the surface of the moon,
unable to release the rover it carried inside,
unable, in fact, to be recovered at all. You might think
that one thing had nothing to do with the other,
but the moon controls the tides, after all,
and even freshwater rivers can feel its gravitational pull.
So, that a fragile turtle born with a defect we don't have a name for
felt the sudden scrape of the moon and,
in a moment of perfect empathy, offered its spirit to the stars
seems perfectly reasonable to me. Six months later,
on the same day Ohioans woke to our mud-covered cars,
the Houston-based company that built Athena
declared that fucked-up mission a success.
Something in that seems logical, too,
in the way we've come to know logic
in this, the good old U S of A.

IV.
Listen: mud seeping so strangely
from ubiquitously gray central Ohio skies
isn't anywhere close to the drones and missiles
raining down on other parts of the world.
But it caught our attention. We thought, if only for a moment,
about one thing causing another,
and that seems like some kind of start
for folks whose stars are forever tied to their stripes.

We've not yet come to the plague of pythons in Florida,
or the plague of measles in Texas sure, like the mud, to spread
to us all, but that's the promise of America:
what goes around comes around. And here we are,
smoke and soot crossing borders of every kind,
sailing the gulf stream, making even Ohioans wonder
what a wall could possibly be for: nothing really,
as the waddling groundhogs in my back yard
could have told you well before this.
But isn't it true about humans that we want to believe
everything happens for a reason?
So why wouldn't mud raining down from the sky
be a plague of its own—a warning sea-cow siren
calling us in from this sea of so much sorrow,
and why wouldn't we want to see that
as something so mythically beautiful
we'll tell our children's children it saved us
and the generations it will take to unravel the unholy mess
we created while calling ourselves the greatest generation
of the greatest nation on Earth? God, the hubris
that got us here, here where it takes a poet like me
to say to readers like you, *I'm so sorry for what we've done.*
Please, forgive us our every trespass,
as it takes a baptism like this—bathed in the filth of our very being—
to clear these styes from our eyes.

Grief as Tunnel Painted on the Side of a Mesa

I review my notes, snatches of dreams
that often turn into poems. Here's one:
> *Jar of Animals. They grow. There are more*
> *than I thought. Parrot's beak snaps off*
> *in my hand. Snake is actually a giraffe.*
> *There's a woman upstairs, fangs out.*

Of this, I remember only the parrot's beak,
black—like a fingernail, maybe,
waiting to fall off. Like a spent blossom.
I can feel the vague echo of the break
between my thumb and forefinger,
the strange stillness of what lay in the palm
of my hand. The fearful thought:
I didn't mean for this to happen.
Who was the woman upstairs, *fangs out*, angry
at me for what I'd done—or offering, perhaps,
what must be plucked from her, too,
what she'd borrowed from the snake
now tall enough to reach her?

I can't remember my dreams anymore.

Other notes tell me:
> *I met Gary Busey on a bus. Conversation*
> *just so good. Witty, sharp. Becomes clear*
> *I'll be spending the night.*

And this:
> *I approach the trail around the lake,*
> *heavy with darkness.*

In that dream, the notes tell me, I can see the moon
in the sky above but follow the sun reflected
on the surface of the water.

More and more, I think, I've been dreaming
of my father, woke last week screaming
I love you! as his face retreated into a darkness

I couldn't reach, a black hole
solid as the one Coyote painted
on the side of a mesa. Somewhere, a road runner:
beep beep! But not tonight I'd guess,
or tomorrow night either, Grief can't be called upon
at will, ordered as if from a menu.
                                    Instead,
sleep brings us a jar full of animals. A beak
that breaks like a breadstick nobody asked for.
And a woman at the top of the stairs, famished maybe,
waiting to fill the hole in her belly, the whole
of her heart, ready to consume what's offered:
guilt, sin, a glass full of sadness. She knows grief
is a jar full of beasts morphing endlessly:
chimera, illusion. But so is love, as far as that goes.
So is fear. She knows fathers never could protect us,
not when they were living, not when snakes nipped
at their own heels, when they knew birds parrot back
only words they hear from us,
and in that strange translation,
they lose all meaning.

The woman upstairs knows Gary Busey
disappointed us all (and Buddy Holly died young,
before he could.) She knows the moon
never leaves us, and that sunlight shimmering
on any body of water will always be a path
worth following. That light mimics light
the same way a tunnel painted on the side of a mesa
mimics a great black hole. That we can enter both
when we're ready. She knows Gary Busey,
young, was a beautiful thing. That I was, too,
and you were, and the trail around even a shimmering lake
eventually ages us all: disease, dementia, decrepitude.
We hold ourselves above the fray, or try to,
fangs out, devouring what's ever been good,
deflecting what we don't need,
knowing one looks just like the other

and so comes back and comes back
and comes back.
Sometimes we enter the tunnel
only to be hit by a train. Sometimes, if we're lucky,
we realize we've always been that bird, beep-beep,
running and running through even a solid black wall,
beak intact, coming through just fine on the other side.

Terms of Venery
Revised for the Ancestors

A purgatory of patriarchy,
a miracle of matriarchs,
a tremble of trust.

What It Is to Feel Small

The spiderwebs in my basement
taste sweet, I learned,
covering my face like a veil
as I sorted through a pile of long-untouched whatnot
stacked in the corner. I barely felt it,
but then licked my lips and tasted something
like a memory of cotton candy.

Later, the aurora borealis sheathed Ohio skies
in its purple veil, and we all remembered
something like wonder. Awe. What it is
to feel small but not forgotten.

Later still—a few days—
as I make my way toward you,
the super moon low on the horizon
conjures the holy Eucharist, ritual
of communion. I hear myself cry out.

This is wonder. Sublime.
That a great sky priest might offer the wafer
memory tells me was dry on the tongue,
stuck, sometimes, to the hard palate,
loosened with a sip of wine
and finally dissolved: *Jesus in the belly,*
the warm glow that followed.

On the Weight of the Soul, the Weight of a Cloud, the Weight of a Whale

A man once said he had proof of the soul,
that it weighed twenty-one grams—less than
a single ounce—and though it wasn't true,
we liked the idea that the soul exists
in quantifiable form. When a child then asked
the weight of a cloud, the innocent expected
a similar answer, that the ethereal nature
of what cloud is would be both calculable
and negligible. And we'd have been wrong.
A single cumulus cloud weighs as much
as two blue whales. A storm cloud even more,
as much as a pod of whales plodding across
the sky. As to the weight of full cloud cover,
any poet can tell you we're back to the weight
of the suffering soul. The only thing keeping us
aloft is the air between the burdens of water,
which is to say, tiny particles of something like
breath, which is to say, *Keep breathing!* Poets
have learned to endure, to sing from the depths
while listening for sounds that mean the pod
has heard, that we're not alone, that the weight
we bear is less than it seems, our stories
weaving a web that holds the sky and the sea
together, the frauds and the faithful believers,
and if we close our eyes, we'll realize we know
the soul is real, that clouds release the weight
of their suffering every day, bathing us
in the beauty of rain that weighs exactly as much
as our tears, exactly as much as the questions
sailing across the sky, the land and the sea,
exactly as much as the answers.

Shadow of the Bird

after Matthew Arnold

The shadow of the bird swept across
the *naked shingles* of the flood plain. Opaque,
barely wavering, defined by the clear, finger-like tips
of his wings: Turkey Vulture. I saw him
before I saw him (against the blue sky / between
the branches of the maple / oak / hackberry trees
all around us). Felt him, really. Knew to look.
It was cool in the dappled shade, comfortable
on the hefty trunk of a fallen tree. What remained
of the barely moving river was solace and memory.
Fear, maybe. A glimpse of what we knew
our future to be. For now, though—
early September—we had only to be here.

Later, following the flood plain back and back
and back into the woods, we came to a clearing.
We'd not been looking for her when we'd set out,
neither joy, nor love, nor light, / nor certitude,
nor peace, nor help for pain, yet found her:
enormous sycamore, holy, emblazoned white
within a strangely beautiful glow of golden light—
the source of that earlier, stealthy shadow—
cascading down. We gazed a while. Witnessed.
Then we left, as all things do.

IV.

Making It Easier

Hold hard then, heart.
This way at least you live.

— Derek Walcott

Aubade

Light seeps in,
even through the room-darkening curtains.
It seeps

around the edges of the window frame. I know
I cannot fend this day off forever.
This day, every day,

seeps
into my dreams, pulling me, still paralyzed,
to consciousness:

the light,
these sheets,
my husband's hand on my hip,
the beauty and joy of the day:
       the sound of the day—
       the dawn chorus—
       the what-will-I-do-with-the-day,
       the what-*must*-I-do-with-the-day,
       the what-won't-I-get done. Again.
The anticipation
of all my new failures.

There will be, of course,
the learning:
       what my failures will teach me.
       Hindsight and revelation:
       epiphany.

But first, first
the awakening. Trying
to determine which world is real—
dreams so detailed
       and real
so eloquent

and real
so terrifying
and real.
Oh, my dreams,
my guides,
my gurus,
my dawn
of understanding.
Oh cruelty
of daylight:
the kidnap, the fight,
my fear of birdsong, of birds—
oh, those clattering birds—
chipping cardinals,
barking crows,
the silent swoop of hawk:
Pay attention.
Not too much attention.

Eventually, I am fully in my body.
Eventually, I am fully sure:
this is the world I must make my way through.

Eventually, I pull the curtain open
and brace for the assault: daylight,
my senses exposed.
I shield my eyes with my hands,
curtain my face,
then caress it,
then pull that curtain, too,

ready
for the beauty and terror of the day that waits,
for what it is
to be alive to this world.

What Feeds / What Is Fed

My sadness, so often, is the sea.
      I flounder. Thrash. Grow tired.
            Understand the depths. Know

            who, before me, was pulled down
      into them, chewed and eaten
by what lives below, by what,

in my thrashing, I try to save
      myself from. One day, suddenly,
            I understood the dead man's float

            was a way to keep myself alive.
      Stop thrashing. Face the depths.
Let the water hold me.

When I needed to breathe,
      I flipped myself over and,
            still supported by the water itself,

            studied the sky. The clouds, I knew,
      were made of water, too,
the life-giving kind,

and when they grow heavy,
      holding too much, they just let go.
            They feed parched lands, weepy marshes,

            feed even the sea which so many, like me,
      feel so lost inside. I kept my eyes
on the clouds, watched them

move into and away from
      each other, turn into faces and animals
            and objects I recognized, and I started

to swim in the direction clouds move,
which is to say, where the wind takes us
all, and finally found the fjords,

the lagoons, inlets that feed into the sea.
Land was within my reach if I just kept
going, cleansed of the salt encrusting my skin,

my hair, the seaweed tangling my toes.
This, I saw, was water that could quench
my thirst, and I swallowed too much,

too much, nearly drowning again
in rivers of so much beauty.
I found a boulder and clung to it, rested,

felt myself saved till the waters thrashed
over us both and I was forced to let go.
I knew I was swimming upstream,

that currents could carry me back
to the sea, so I looked for the tributaries
and entered them, found when I stopped

to tread the water, I could sometimes feel
a sandy bottom. I could sometimes stand.
I could drink without drowning. Here

was the shade of the sycamores. Here
was the grandeur of an Earth nourished
by water, who drinks from the rooted

soil, who bows its head to the falling
rain. Here, in the tributaries, I understood
meandering, moderation, slowing down

without stopping, and traveling
           without tears. Here, in the tributaries,
                      I understand what it means to be nourished:

                      to be fed and to feed in a cycle that moves
           in perpetual, perfect motion. Sometimes,
yes, I climb ashore. Sometimes, still,

I float back to the sea, now trusting
           it has its own beauty, that it has its own power
                      and place. That the beasts below need to be

                      left alone, and other beasts need to be
           saved. I spend my time now mostly
in the tributaries. Giving, taking,

breathing in what comes
           from the sky. Floating, turning,
                      digging in, learning over and over to let go.

Making It Easier

Tired, still recovering—
though you tested negative a week ago—
you watch old episodes of *Columbo*.

Through the window behind the TV
a single pink bud opens slowly
on the tulip magnolia in the yard.

Your eyes shift back and forth:
the murderess, both *lady lawyer*
and evil stepmother, pilots a plane

in a silk scarf and yellow aviators.
Columbo's glass eye, you decide,
is on the right; it never moves.

He opens a suitcase full of money
that proves the woman is guilty,
can't find a dollar to pay the waitress.

Outside, the tree is full of buds,
tiny, stubborn, pink fists, that one
chiffon blossom opening to the fading

sun, fluttering, just a little,
in the breeze. There's no moral
to the story—this one, I mean. Earlier,

at the doctor's office, the nurse
lifted your breast to place the leads
for the EKG. You lay on the table

too tired to be embarrassed or to help.
She lifts the breast again, places another
lead, all while smiling and telling you

a story of her own. No villain.
No hero. Just something that happened
last week, something to make this feel

ordinary, no big deal, not piloting
a plane while looking stunning,
not solving a crime no one else can.

Just talking, making it easier for you
to relax and to notice, later, a fist
unfolding, which is no small miracle.

On Making Banana Bread the Day Before My Mother's Surgery

I cracked an egg into a cup, saw flecks of blood
and the embryo a few days old.

My mother taught me this—to crack the egg separately
before adding it to the batter.

Seeing the little gray comma, its black eye spot,
I was grateful…and a little bit sick.

Later, when I pulled the bread from the oven,
I knew it didn't look right. I sliced it:

pale, dry, no flavor. It took a minute
for me to realize that, so concerned was I for the egg,

I'd never added the fruit: sad, speckled,
and still on the counter. I threw the bread out

before deciding what to do with the egg
still in its cup. It sat there all day.

Somewhere after midnight, I poured it into the sink,
watched it slither down the drain.

My mother would never have waited so long.
What's done is done, she'd say. *The past is past.*

It was never clear exactly how one handles the future—
except, I guess, to deal with what comes.

I let the water run a while, turned on the disposal,
winced. In the morning, when I got the call

that mom was okay, I fully sanitized the sink
while I cried through the precipice of that lost egg,

the wasted bread, and the bananas I'd put in the fridge
and still had to reckon with now.

What Was and Wasn't

The wind is blowing hard.
        From where I sit, blue skies
and billowing clouds

        through one window,
bleak gray drear
        through another. Already,

as I write this, the wind
        has won, blue skies now
all around, clarifying

        details of every tree limb
glowing with the shape
        and sheen of pale green buds

at their tangled tips.
        Small miracle. Last night,
I dreamed of you.

        Your dimly lit house
suddenly bright
        and cheerful. You were

bright and cheerful,
        and I was. The winds
of change, I guess,

        clarify everything:
what was and wasn't.
        What is. What needn't be.

You were cooking,
        stirring a pot and smiling.
You lifted the spoon

toward me and smiled:
Try this! I woke, wary,
      conflicted, that shifting

wind working
      so hard. I sat still
and quiet: watching,

      listening, aware that
the drear has moved on
      to someone else, will return

to me in time.
      Suddenly grasping
the secret of miracles.

Redbuds

On the way there, an enormous deer
    on the side of the road covered in black vultures,
        one in Horaltic pose. Earlier, on my way to the car,

I'd seen his text: *There's been a decline.*
    Thought I should warn you. When I arrive,
        she's freshly shorn: a new haircut. Eyes bright,

frames of her glasses enhanced
    by the color of a new, nubby-red sweater.
        Hello there! she says, and I show her pictures

of what's blooming in the yard,
    my granddaughter in eclipse glasses
        over a paper plate mask. We have a grand time.

On the way home, redbud trees—
    more than I've ever seen—are blossoming
        on Riverside Drive. The water, springtime-high,

moves brusquely along. The sky
    is a wide expanse of blue, stirred by vultures
        aloft on lazy currents, satiated for now and in no hurry.

Hydrangeas

In the yard today, I watched a cardinal zigzag
down the length of the fence, eyeing either side
for greener grass, maybe, or the choicest insects,

and as he dropped down the other side,
disappearing altogether, I was left to assume
my neighbor's healthier clover. I tried not to feel

lonesome, though—truth told—not being chosen
hurt somehow, the way that kind of thing does
for introverts. *Maybe that cardinal was an introvert*

too, I hear my father say. I hear his voice quite a lot
these days, maybe because he skimmed down
either side of a certain fence himself not long ago:

life, death. It could have gone either way.
But the bright flame of his body disappeared, too.
Greener pastures—all that. The yard without us

in it. And I mean, plenty of birds still sing over here,
on this side of the fence. I keep cutting hydrangeas,
bringing a new little bit of the outside inside.

Making the house look like a place you might want
to stay for a while, just one more cup of coffee.
One more song, maybe, to soothe the hollow bones.

Ode to Understanding

American Robin, juvenile,
dead in my driveway—left, I suppose,
by the neighbor's cat
who likes to lounge in the shade
beneath my car.
It was a day or two before I saw her,
really saw her, as more
than a dark clump of weed
or piece of litter blown from the recycling
picked up on Wednesday.
                                    It's Friday
and I'd pulled my car up just enough
to finally see what it was,
beautiful bird, eyes gone,
white belly speckled brown
and blushed auburn, slender black legs
stretched into slender black toes
tipped with tiny, terrifying talons.
Her wings fell like a cape
from drooped shoulders,
blending into beautiful tail —
a self-made shroud, waist adorned
with the Tiffany-style brooch
of an emerald fly with ruby eyes.
                                    I confess:
I keep a small album of dead-bird photos
on my phone, each deathbed portrait
a study in elegance, the details we don't see
when a bird common as a robin
flits and flies overhead, tree to lawn to tree,
fattening through winter, slender in spring,
there, always there, always there,
like so many other things we take for granted
but appreciate when they're gone.
Like parents. Like angry children.
Like prayer. And breath. And the lingering notes
of a long-forgotten, favorite song.

Peonies

Between rains, the mowers
finally come. After, grackles

cover the lawn: hungry, fed,
delighted. The wind blows

lightly through the peonies
whispering, *It will all be okay.*

Apocalypse

Just as ocean holds her arms open
to the melting glacier,
just as air so wildly embraces fire
that sky might waltz with the smoke,
just as hillsides tumble and slide
in their haste to kiss the unmoving surface
of the valley, and sinkholes
rend themselves open to the void,
so you, in your sublime terror—
drowning, burning, giving in to gravity
and the vast emptiness of mystical love—
see sacred singularity at last. Oneness.
Wholeness. What the sandy particles
of stardust were sent here to grasp.

And If I Should Die by the Same Strain That Killed My Avian Brethren, Let Them Not Say

she said so, though I did.
Let them say instead, *Listen to her now*

for the words still stand:
We are the same, feathered, un-feathered,

scaled and so on, for when the un-feathered beasts
released from the leaden weight of human form

passed on to the pale-gold light of angels,
each one said, *I see it now.*

I understand. And it was not too late
for, lo, the un-winged now winged chant beside us all:

Listen. Listen. Listen.
The hum of that low chorus—do you hear it?—

has always told us what we should do:
listen, listen, to the thrum of human hearts

in time with sap running through trees,
and birds' migrating wings,

and whales' thunderously splashing tales,
and the ants marching in formation,

and the snore of bees resting in flowering buds
as they grow tired from carrying so much sweetness,

and as they wake and return to the hive,
and as we the collective hive process it all

and the cycle starts over and over again
orchestrated by the wind which does not end—

not when sirens wail, not when we take no notice at all
of the sound and scent and splash and buzz

of this planet spinning its way through the sky.
So when the birds die, and the bovine herds,

and when we humans die mid-thrust and -parry and -slash
of our swords, and when the insects starve

and grasses wither, and when the oceans evaporate entirely
into deserts of plastic trash-island waste,

and the last strain of the last virus wriggles and spins
through its own final death throe,

let the silence be silent, pulsing and pealing
as it has all along: *Listen. Listen. Listen.*

Apologia

Whatever mistakes I've made
in my life, let them be forgiven
for the planting of milkweed.

May whomever I've wronged
understand I did what I could
to help the birds, the whales,

my every neighbor and child.
Whatever mistakes I've made,
understand I meant to be kind,

to help, to honor the lesser gods
forgotten, in need of praise
and their own celebration.

This Is Why the Patter of Rain

Red-winged blackbird, wings aflame
and dizzy with joy, asks us to see all that he sees:
sunrise, the intricate patterns of light and shadow
quivering through every bush and every tree
till nightfall—and rain! Slick, tasty,
making mud of the world.
                                Hear it? Patter, rush,
thunder? Even when it doesn't rain—dew?
How the air itself swells to visible sparkle?
Don't get him started on wind: breeze, gale,
the tingling it brings to the body.
How it holds us aloft.

Old crow, charred, grunts and barks
her affirmation: I've been saying this for years,
that light is a miracle, that rain to a parched mouth
is sweet as honey. That darkness is a gift—
every night sky offering a velvet tray of stars
we couldn't see sparkling in the day,
though they're there.
                                And snow, sometimes,
like a trillion stars falling at once, sending
the world into stunned, silent glee.

Old crow knows what the young and trilling
red-winged blackbird thinks he's just discovered.
Crow's been singing that song so many years
her voice is raw, reduced to a single, hoarse syllable:
Caw! Red-winged blackbird doesn't trust crow—
nor should he. Crow watches his nest
too carefully. Old crow, hungry crow—
                                noisy crow!
She scans the sky for hawk, heron, crane. Scans
the grass for fox, snake, weasel. Knows that hunger
is a kind of beauty—that she'd swallow the snow
and stars if she could, swallow the sun and shadows.

So would hawk, whose belly—soft, brown, speckled—
is fed by the very thing that bloodies his talons.

This is why the patter of rain washing us clean
cries in cracks of thunder, why the sun
sometimes burns. Why the morning dew
gently recalls what seeps from every wound.
The breeze whispers contrition and gales
beg for forgiveness—and the very wings
of a red-winged blackbird pulse with love
while they also flash their warning. Old crow
rides the wind like he does, like hawk does.
She feels herself dizzy with joy, like he does,
hawk does, like the sun and rain and shadow,
the stars and snow, heron, crane, fox, weasel,
and the tingling that hunger brings to the body.

Paula J. Lambert has published four previous full-length poetry collections including *As If This Did Not Happen Every Day* (Sheila-Na-Gig Editions 2024). She has authored six chapbooks, including *Sinkhole* (Bottlecap Press 2025). Lambert, also a literary translator, was awarded the 2021 PEN America—L'Engle Rahman Prize for Mentorship. Her work has been supported by the Ohio Arts Council, the Greater Columbus Arts Council, and the Virginia Center for Creative Arts. She is the 2023 winner of the *Slippery Elm* Poetry Prize and the New England Poetry Club's Amy Lowell Prize, was awarded a 2021 Editor's Choice Award from *Sheila-Na-Gig online*, and was the 2019 winner of the *Heartland* Broadside Series. Lambert owns Full/Crescent Press, a small publisher of poetry books and broadsides, through which she has founded and supported numerous public readings and festivals that support the intersection of poetry and science, including the Sun & Moon Festival now hosted by the Ohio Poetry Association. She lives in Columbus with her husband, Dr. Michael Perkins, a philosopher and technologist. More at www.paulajlambert.com.

Sheila-Na-Gig Editions